W9-ATF-179

Predators

# Lions
## on the Hunt

Alicia Z. Klepeis

Lerner Publications ◆ Minneapolis

Content Consultant: Bruce D. Leopold, PhD, Department of Wildlife and Fisheries,
Mississippi State University

Lerner Publications Company
A division of Lerner Publishing Group, Inc.
241 First Avenue North
Minneapolis, MN 55401 USA

For reading levels and more information, look up this title at
www.lernerbooks.com.

Library of Congress Cataloging-in-Publication Data

Names: Klepeis, Alicia, 1971–
Title: Lions on the hunt / by Alicia Z. Klepeis.
Description: Minneapolis : Lerner Publications, [2018] | Series: Searchlight
   books. Predators | Audience: Age 8–11. | Audience: Grade 4 to 6. |
   Includes bibliographical references and index.
Identifiers: LCCN 2016054415 (print) | LCCN 2017008455 (ebook) | ISBN
   9781512433951 (lb : alk. paper) | ISBN 9781512456103 (pb : alk. paper) |
   ISBN 9781512450811 (eb pdf)
Subjects:  LCSH: Lion—Juvenile literature.
Classification: LCC QL737.C23 K5925 2018 (print) | LCC QL737.C23 (ebook) |
   DDC 599.757--dc23

LC record available at https://lccn.loc.gov/2016054415

Manufactured in the United States of America
1 — CG — 7/15/17

Contents

# Chapter 1

# ON THE HUNT

It's evening on the African savanna. A gentle breeze sweeps through the tall grass. A lioness raises her head from the grass where she is resting. She sniffs deeply, catching a whiff of wildebeests. A watering hole lies in the distance. A herd of thirsty wildebeests is drinking. Their tongues lap the cool water. Some are full-grown. Others are young.

The lioness spots its prey and will join other lions to hunt. Why might lions hunt together?

The lioness is hungry. So is the rest of the pride. A pride of lions is a group that lives and hunts together. Hunting together helps them take down large prey. The lionesses in the pride look for a sick or old wildebeest that will be easier to kill, though they will hunt a healthy animal too. They spot one with an injured leg.

The lionesses waste no time. They are ready for action. A few lionesses stalk through the grass. With their padded paws, they move almost silently. They creep closer and closer to where the wildebeests are drinking.

**The lionesses creep toward the herd, looking for its weakest member.**

A lion's powerful jaws help it kill prey.

## The Hunt

The other lionesses spread out in a fan-shaped formation.  Some of them head directly for the prey. This forces the injured wildebeest to make its way toward the grass where the lionesses are waiting.  The other wildebeests make a hasty retreat.

When the lone wildebeest is close, three lionesses bolt out of hiding.  They bite and scratch the wildebeest. They surround and pin the prey so it can't escape.  One lioness bites down, and the wildebeest struggles before it goes completely still.

# Male Lions as Hunters

While the lionesses do most of the hunting, male lions are also good hunters. But they are not as fast at chasing down prey. They are heavier and less agile than female lions. Males are also less likely to cooperate with other lions when hunting. Yet because of their greater size and strength, male lions kill larger prey than lionesses. They tend to ambush their prey in areas with dense vegetation like tall grass.

A male lion attacks a bull buffalo.

Male lions get first choice of meat once the prey is killed.

Soon all the male lions in the pride arrive at the kill. The lionesses back away while the males fight over the animal's carcass, or dead body. The lions snarl and claw at one another to get their share of the meat. They eat until they have had their fill.

Next, the hunters get their turn. The females feed on what remains of the wildebeest. Finally, the lion cubs eat. After the meal, the lions lick themselves clean and groom one another. They return to the tall grass to sleep. It has been a successful hunt.

# Chapter 2

# WHERE LIONS LIVE

In the past, African lions lived in many places. Their range spread from northern Africa to the tip of South Africa. It also stretched to southwest Asia and into Europe and India. These days, the African lions' range is limited to south of the Sahara Desert in what is called sub-Saharan Africa.

Many lions live near zebras and wildebeests. Where do lions live?

Most lions live on the African savannas. These flat grasslands have few trees. The weather is hot and dry. Little rain falls here. Lions share the savannas with many other animals, including zebras and antelope. Lions also live and hunt in open woodlands.

Lions are very important in the ecosystems where they live. They are apex predators, which means they are at the top of the food chain. Lions keep one species from taking over an ecosystem. Without lions to eat grazing animals such as antelope and wildebeests, these grazers could eat up all the savannas' grasses. This would turn the land into a desert.

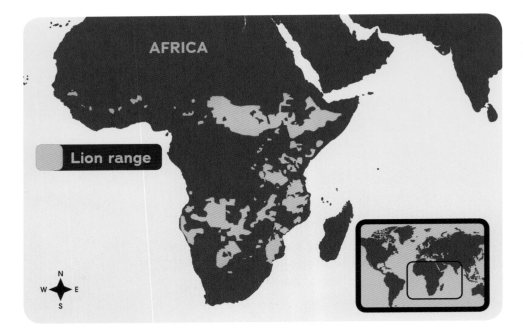

AFRICA

Lion range

N
W E
S

# Lion Territories

The area where a lion pride lives is called its territory. A territory varies in size depending on how much prey is available. A 100-square-mile (259-square-kilometer) territory is common. To be successful hunters, lions must know their territory well. They remember where the watering holes are and where their prey hangs out. They know where good ambush spots are located.

Watering holes are a good place to find prey.

# Population

Scientists estimate that in 2016, only 23,000 to 39,000 adult African lions lived in the wild. These numbers are dropping. The biggest threat to lions is humans. Killing lions and moving their hides to other countries is illegal in many places. But people hunt them anyway.

Habitat loss also affects lions. People destroy lions' territory when they clear land for agriculture, settlements, and roads. Lions lose plants they used for hunting cover, making hunting more difficult. These changes also get rid of plants that the lions' prey eat. When the prey leave, lions lose their traditional food sources.

Roads bring humans closer to lions. This can be dangerous for both humans and lions.

ASIATIC LIONS TEND TO HAVE
SHORTER, DARKER MANES THAN
AFRICAN LIONS.

Not all lions live in Africa. Asiatic lions live in only one place in the world: the Gir Forest of northwestern India. These lions typically eat deer. There are estimated to be fewer than five hundred Asiatic lions left in the wild.

# Chapter 3

# POWERFUL PREDATORS

Lions are big cats. Only the tiger is larger. Lions stand from 3.5 to 4 feet (1 to 1.2 meters) tall at the shoulder. Females can be up to 9 feet (2.7 m) long, and males get up to 10 feet (3 m) long. That is as long as a basketball hoop is high. Females weigh up to 395 pounds (180 kilograms), and males can weigh up to 550 pounds (250 kg). The end of a lion's tail is tufted.

Lions are large cats, but which cat is larger than a lion?

Lions are good sprinters. They can run at 35 miles (55 km) per hour. But they can keep that speed for only a few seconds.

Lions' fur ranges from light yellow to a darker brown. These colors allow them to blend in with the savanna's long, dry grass. Lions have two coats of fur. A lighter underlayer keeps extreme heat and cold from reaching the lion's skin. The outer layer of fur is made up of wiry guard hairs. This layer protects the lion from thorns, rain, and other animals' claws.

**A lion's coloring makes it harder for prey to spot.**

# The Mane Attraction

Lions are the only cat species with manes. Only male lions have them. This bushy hair around the lion's neck and head serves many purposes. It shows that a male lion is healthy and fit. It warns other males that the well-maned beast is strong and capable of fighting.

**A male lion's mane protects it during fights.**

## Hunting Tools

Lions have great eyesight. In the dark, they can see six times better than people. Sometimes it looks as if light is shining off a lion's eyes. Lions have a special layer of reflective cells at the back of their eyes. When moonlight or starlight hits these cells, the light bounces forward. This illuminates what is in front of them to help them see in the dark, as a car's headlights do. Lions also have excellent hearing. They can hear prey up to 1 mile (1.5 km) away.

The reflective surface in a lion's eye is called the tapetum lucidum.

Lions use their
claws to catch prey.

Lions use their sharp claws to grab and hold down prey. The claws can be retracted, or pulled back, when they are not in use. This keeps the claws from wearing down too fast or getting caught on things.

Lions' teeth also make them terrific hunters. Lions have 30 teeth, all of which are useful for killing and eating meat. Four long, curved canine teeth allow the lion to hold its prey in place, kill it, and tear it apart. Each canine is nearly 4 inches (10 centimeters) long!

Lions also have four carnassial teeth located under both of their cheeks. The carnassial teeth act as scissors, cutting meat. These teeth can carve through prey's tendons and tough skin. Lions don't have any teeth that are good for chewing, so they swallow their food in chunks.

The carnassial teeth are at the very back of a lion's mouth. They are the sharpest teeth.

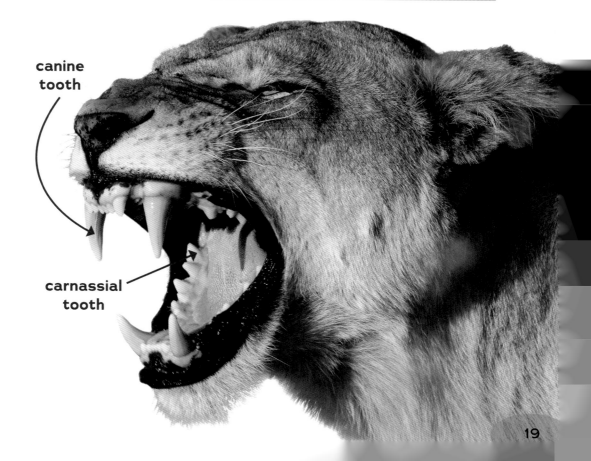

canine tooth

carnassial tooth

# Chapter 4

# HOW LIONS BEHAVE

People often think of lions as fierce and ferocious killers. But lions are also very social animals. Some prides have only a few members, while others have as many as forty lions. Lions are particularly social after they eat. When they finish eating, the lions in a pride groom each other. This strengthens relationships within the pride.

Two male lions groom each other. Why do lions groom one another?

A pride has only a few adult males.  Males in a pride may be brothers or cousins.  These males have often killed other males to take charge.  When new male lions take over a pride, they kill any cubs that are not their own.  Then they father cubs with the females in the pride. Males typically remain in charge of a pride for two to three years before being kicked out or killed themselves. Those kicked out of prides live alone or with a few other male lions.  They may try to take over another pride later.

**Female lions outnumber male lions in a pride.**

A male lion's main job in a pride is to defend the pride's territory. Male lions roar to tell other lions to stay away. A lion's roar can be heard from 5 miles (8 km) away. A lioness may also roar to warn her cubs of danger.

A LION'S ROAR IS ABOUT TWENTY-FIVE TIMES LOUDER THAN A GAS-POWERED LAWN MOWER.

Young cubs stay close to their mothers.

Female lions in a pride are usually related. They are grandmothers, mothers, sisters, aunts, or daughters. As female lions grow up, they tend to stay with their pride. They help raise new cubs and hunt for food. When male lions get big enough to compete with the dominant males of the pride, they head out to look for a new pride to join.

# The Lion Life Cycle

Lions are able to reproduce when they are between three and four years old, and they breed any time of year. A lioness gives birth to two to four cubs, which nurse until they are seven to nine months old. The mother lion may play games with her cubs, flicking her tail to get them to practice pouncing and stalking prey. Cubs join the hunt when they are around eleven months old.

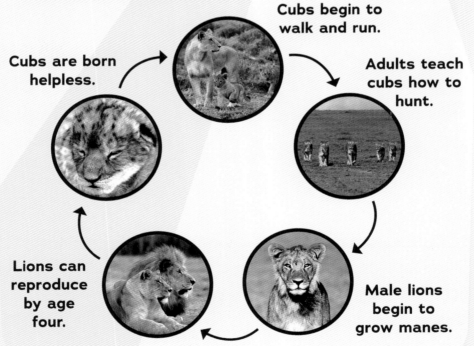

Cubs begin to walk and run.

Adults teach cubs how to hunt.

Cubs are born helpless.

Lions can reproduce by age four.

Male lions begin to grow manes.

## Diet and Strategies

Prides spend a few hours hunting, about one hour eating, and twenty hours sleeping each day. Lions rest to save their energy for the hunt. They often rest out in the open. Lions are not worried about other animals hurting them because they are apex predators where they live.

Lions are carnivores. They have been known to eat any nearby animal, including ostriches and reptiles. Sometimes lions hear wild dogs, hyenas, or other animals eating. They creep in to steal these animals' food. A lion gets up to half its food by stealing. Few animals would fight a lion to keep a meal.

**Lions lose an attempt to steal food only when there are more hyenas than lions.**

**Lions hide in tall grass as they creep toward prey.**

Lions have even been seen eating whale carcasses that washed up on African beaches. They drink water when it is available but can obtain all the moisture they need from their prey.

Excellent hunting strategies keep lions at the top of the food chain. They are skilled at sneaking up on prey. The pads under their toes allow them to walk almost silently. Lions on the hunt often hide quietly among vegetation and wait for prey. This is called ambush hunting.

Members of a pride work together to hunt. Lionesses frequently hunt in groups of two or three. Together, they stalk, trap, and kill their prey. Even if a single lion could easily take down an impala, hunting in teams makes it easier to detect, corner, and kill larger prey.

Lions are incredibly powerful predators. They are capable of killing huge animals such as giraffes, wildebeests, and buffalo. Lions' strength and hunting skills have no rival in the African savannas.

**Several lions can take down larger prey than just one lion can.**

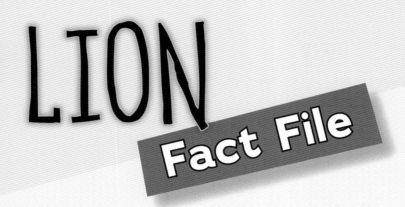

# LION

## Fact File

**Scientific Name:** *Panthera leo*

**Where It Is Found:** many parts of sub-Saharan Africa

**Habitat:** grassland, desert, open woodlands

**Diet:** zebras, antelopes, wildebeests

**Height:** 3.5 to 4 feet (1–1.2 m)

**Length:** Males are up to 10 feet (3 m) long, and females are up to 9 feet (2.7 m) long.

**Weight:** Males weigh 330 to 550 pounds (150–250 kg). Females weigh 265 to 395 pounds (120–180 kg).

**Life Span:** 15 to 18 years in the wild

# Food Chain

# Glossary

**ambush:** a surprise attack made from a hidden position

**apex predator:** an animal that has no natural predators and is at the top of a food chain

**carnivore:** an animal that eats meat

**ecosystem:** a community of plants, animals, and other organisms and their environment

**habitat:** a place where an animal naturally lives

**prey:** animals that other animals hunt and eat

**pride:** a group of lions that lives and travels together

**savanna:** a grassland in eastern Africa with few, scattered trees

**tendon:** a part of a body that attaches muscles to bones

**territory:** a defended area of land

**wildebeest:** a large African antelope with a long head, short mane, and sloping back

# Learn More about Lions

## Books

Blewett, Ashlee Brown. *Mission: Lion Rescue: All about Lions and How to Save Them*. Washington, DC: National Geographic Kids Books, 2014. This book describes challenges lions face in the wild and how people can help these big cats.

Downer, Ann. *Wild Animal Neighbors: Sharing Our Urban World*. Minneapolis: Twenty-First Century Books, 2014. Learn why animals are moving into cities and how people can coexist with their animal neighbors.

Pope, Kristen. *On the Hunt with African Lions*. Mankato, MN: Child's World, 2016. Discover the lives of African lions, including their behavior and how they hunt.

## Websites

**National Geographic: Lions Hunting**
http://video.nationalgeographic.com/video/lion_african_hunting?
Watch a lion pride hunt a wildebeest, and learn about the advantages and disadvantages lions have when hunting.

**National Geographic Kids: Lion**
http://kids.nationalgeographic.com/animals/lion/#lion-male-roar.jpg
This website gives an overview of lions, including how they hunt, where they live, and how big they are.

**Zoo Atlanta: African Lion**
http://www.zooatlanta.org/african_lion
Read fun facts about lions, as well as details on the life cycle and lifestyle of these big cats.

# Index

# Photo Acknowledgments

The images in this book are used with the permission of: © Papa Bravo/Shutterstock.com, p. 4;
© Uwe Skrzypczak/ImageBroker RM/Glow Images, p. 5; © Seyms Brugger/Shutterstock.com,
p. 6; © Aoosthuizen/iStock.com, p. 7; © Patrick_Gijsbers/iStock.com, p. 8; © 1001slide/iStock.com,
p. 9; © Red Line Editorial, p. 10; © MylesP/Shutterstock.com, p. 11; © Four Oaks/Shutterstock.com,
p. 12; © Andrea Izzotti/Shutterstock.com, p. 13; © lrosebrugh/iStock.com, p. 14; © Honey Cloverz/
Shutterstock.com, p. 15; © J_K/Shutterstock.com, p. 16; © Erwin Niemand/Shutterstock.com,
p. 17; © Jez Bennett/Shutterstock.com, p. 18; © swakopphoto.com/Shutterstock.com, p. 19;
© Kenneth Canning/iStock.com, p. 20; © BrettDurrant/iStock.com, p. 21; © Dr Ajay Kumar Singh/
Shutterstock.com, p. 22; © prasit_chansareekorn/iStock.com, pp. 23, 24 (top); © Yungsu/
iStock.com, p. 24 (middle left); © Maggy Meyer/iStock.com, p. 24 (middle right); © Tony Camacho/
Science Source, p. 24 (bottom right); © hoschi/iStock.com, p. 24 (bottom left); © Clem Haagner/
Science Source, p. 25; © Alta Oosthuizen/Shutterstock.com, p. 26; © DextairPhotography/
Shutterstock.com, p. 27; © Eric Isselee/Shutterstock.com, pp. 29 (top), 29 (middle right); © prapass/
Shutterstock.com, p. 29 (middle left); © PietroPazzi/iStock.com, p. 29 (bottom).

Front Cover: © Rgbe/Dreamstime.com.

Main body text set in Adrianna Regular 14/20.
Typeface provided by Chank.